Loge Liberté chérie
A Light in the Darkness

Alexander P. Herbert

The views or opinions expressed in this book, and the context in which the images are used, do not necessarily reflect the views or policy of, nor imply approval or endorsement by, the United States Holocaust Memorial Museum.

Copyright © 2020 Alexander P. Herbert

All rights reserved.

ISBN: 9781703690514

To all poor and distressed Freemasons, wheresoever dispersed over the face of earth and water, wishing them a speedy relief from all their sufferings and a safe return to their native country, should they so desire it.

For Kev.

CONTENTS

Preface		i
Introduction		1
1	Culture War	6
2	Night and Fog	23
3	The Priests of Esterwegen	37
4	*Loge Liberté chérie*	56
5	Remembrance	74
Epilogue		85
Bibliography		90
Attributions		97

PREFACE

This book began many years ago when I came across a very brief mention of Masonic Lodges operating during the Holocaust. I don't consider myself prone to hyperbole, but I quickly came to consider this the most important story in the history of Freemasonry. Unfortunately, due to barriers in language and jurisdiction, it hasn't been available to a wide enough audience. When I have found this story presented in English, it was invariably fraught with inaccuracies and circular references.

To correct this, I've spent the past several years collecting and translating primary source materials, particularly eyewitness accounts, and what unfolded was much more than I ever anticipated. Scattered notes slowly but steadily took shape and, after all this time, I've finally admitted to myself that this work has grown from a simple paper to a small book. I also believe that this story deserves (and even demands) more than to be tucked away in a Masonic research journal.

I must start with two general disclaimers.

First, the primary sources mostly agree to a common narrative, but they are often inconsistent in the fine details. At times they even contradict themselves internally. This is the nature of eyewitness accounts from unique, human perspectives. There are three key eyewitnesses, who shared their personal accounts both in autobiographical texts and through interviews provided to other authors. In general, when these accounts disagree, the two that concur are presented over the third that does not. Thus, the story told in this book has largely been self-selected for the clearest, most consistent version of events.

Second, I acknowledge that I am merely a collector and cataloguer of facts. The true work in championing *Loge Liberté chérie* has been accomplished by the faithfulness of her members and many other celebrated authors, references to which follow. I owe a debt of gratitude to several of them for their selfless generosity of research, photographs, and advice – particularly to Frank Langenaken of the *Centre d'Études et de Documentation Maçonniques* (CEDOM)[1], Danny Delcambre of BEL-MEMORIAL, Bastian Salier of Salier Verlag, Pierre Guelff, and Emmanuel Everarts.

I am also thankful to the Ohio Lodge of Research and to Castle Island Virtual Lodge № 190 A.F.&A.M. for providing me early opportunities to share this story and for their valuable feedback, and to the Royal Scofield Society for reigniting my love of writing. Finally, I am indebted to my wife, Meaghan, for her support and for sharing the gift of her artwork, to Renee, Tzara, and Dan for all of their assistance, and to Chad for his ceaseless encouragement.

---

[1] The Center of Masonic Studies and Documentation.

INTRODUCTION

Within popular culture, Freemasonry is seldom far removed from either politics or religion. The mystery that purposefully surrounds the Fraternity easily lends itself to the creation of conspiracy theories – many without merit, but some with unfortunate historical precedent. The arguments made against it by religious groups, and particularly the Catholic Church, are also close to the surface of the pool of common knowledge.

Freemasons are known to both revel in and quickly dismiss these fanciful stories. However, it cannot be denied that Freemasonry has attracted the membership of many powerful men over its long history, and indeed counts many well-known historical figures among its number. It is unlikely that you could venture far beyond the front door of an American Lodge without encountering a large painting of George Washington in Masonic regalia. Freemasons have ruled the world's mightiest countries, have led men in humanity's most terrible wars, and have left their footprints on the Moon.

Why should there not, then, be Lodges that themselves drive great social and political change? What better vehicle could there be to improve society on a grand scale?

For all of this potential, discussion of religious and political topics within the Lodge is largely forbidden by the Fraternity, particularly in the branch found in England and the former British Empire. *The Constitutions of the Free-Masons*, compiled by Dr. James Anderson and first published in 1723 as one of the foundational documents of the newborn Grand Lodge of London and Westminster, includes the following admonition:

> A *Mason is oblig'd by his Tenure, to obey the moral Law ; and if he rightly understands the Art, he will never be a stupid Atheist[2], nor an irreligious Libertine. But though in ancient Times Masons were charg'd in every Country to be of the Religion of that Country or Nation, whatever it was, yet 'tis now thought more expedient only to oblige them to that Religion in which all Men agree, leaving their particular Opinions to themselves ; that is, to be good Men and true, or Men of Honour and Honesty, by whatever Denominations or Persuasions they may be distinguish'd ;* **whereby Masonry becomes the Center of Union, and the Means of conciliating true Friendship among Persons that must else have remain'd at a perpetual Distance.**

[…]

---

[2] The word "stupid" is used not as a base insult, but as the root of the word "stupor" to describe someone who is numb or does not fully sense the world around him.

You may enjoy yourself with innocent Mirth, treating one another according to Ability, but avoiding all Excess, or forcing any Brother to eat or drink beyond his Inclination, or hindering him from going when his Occasions call him, or doing or saying anything offensive, or that may forbid an easy and free Conversation for that would blast our Harmony, and defeat our laudable Purposes. **Therefore no private Piques or Quarrels must be brought within the Door of the Lodge, far less any Quarrels about Religion, or Nations, or State Policy,** *we being only, as Masons, of the Catholick Religion[3] above mention'd, we are also of all Nations, Tongues, Kindreds, and Languages, and are resolv'd against all Politics, as what never yet conduct'd to the Welfare of the Lodge, nor ever will.*

There are two reasons for this prohibition, for which Anderson's Constitutions provides some background. The first is that a Masonic Lodge is supposed to be a place of harmony between its members. Freemasonry entered public perception in the aftermath of great conflicts in England – between Catholics and Protestants, between Parliamentarians and Royalists, etc. – and contemporary Freemasons wanted their Fraternity to remain a safe space where these contentious opinions and issues could be left at the door and its members could focus instead on what they had in common.

The second reason is that the forefathers of the Fraternity recognized and appreciated the terrible

---

[3] The use of the word "Catholick" refers to its traditional definition of "shared" or "mutually agreed upon" and is not a reference to Roman Catholicism.

danger of organized sociopolitical action. Freemasonry quickly spread as merchants, soldiers, and dignitaries carried it around the globe, resulting in a large network of loosely-affiliated Masonic jurisdictions. They were united by a common history and shared ancestors, but found themselves in vastly different cultures. The activities of one jurisdiction could (and, indeed, did) color the public perception of the entire Fraternity and a bad reputation developed in one area of the world could later harm its members in another. It was wisely decided to leave matters of activism to the professionals.

This does not mean that Freemasons must be completely inert. History is filled with men of great purpose, who were also Freemasons. This does not come as a surprise to members of the Fraternity, for its tenets of Brotherly Love towards all humanity, Relief for the misfortunate, and Truth in personal beliefs and actions are commonly found in these most uncommon of men.

Freemasonry provides an opportunity for all men to explore these values and put them into meaningful practice in their individual, personal lives. This can be explained in no better words than those written by Gabriel Jagush:

> *The world is an awful place, and there's not much that we can do about that on the macro scale. What we can do, however, is give men the opportunity to change and improve themselves using moral tools and teachings centered around love of God and love of one another in order to better implement the moral values they already had. By doing this, a man not only changes himself, but the world immediately around him - and sometimes reaching even*

further than that. So, we can't change the world on a macro scale, but we can change it many, many times on a micro scale. **Masonry is an organized effort to save the world through love, one man at a time.**

A man's personal philosophy is easily built to be virtuous when everything in life is going well. His true character, however, is revealed through his choices and actions when his world comes crashing down around him. It is therefore fitting that the most beautiful work of Freemasonry was wrought in the midst of the most hellish conditions imaginable.

CULTURE WAR

The roots of this story begin in the aftermath of the Napoleonic Wars, when the European continent was marked by a period of conflict between civil government and the Church. Secularism was on the rise, an echo of the earlier Enlightenment movement that ended in the bloodbath of the French Revolution. The Holy Roman Empire had been dismantled following the abdication of Holy Roman Emperor Francis II, defeated by Napoleon at the "Battle of the Three Emperors" at Austerlitz. Civil government began reserving many powers and privileges and, as a result, the traditional influence of the Catholic Church was waning. In 1832, Pope Gregory XVI condemned this "liberalism and religious indifferentism" in *Mirani vos:*

> *...the discipline sanctioned by the Church must never be rejected or be branded as contrary to certain principles of natural law. It must never be called crippled, or imperfect or subject to civil authority. In this discipline the*

administration of sacred rites, standards of morality, and the reckoning of the rights of the Church and her ministers are embraced.

Pope Pius IX reaffirmed this stance in his 1864 encyclical *Quanta cura*. An attached Syllabus of Common Errors listed 80 errors of social, political, and religious philosophies that were seen as afflicting contemporary society. This included, specifically, that *"the Church ought to be separated from the State, and the State from the Church"* (Proposition 55).

In 1868, Pope Pius IX convened the First Vatican Council (Vatican I) and two resultant Constitutions were published in 1870. *Pastor aeternus*, the First Dogmatic Constitution on the Church of Christ, established as dogma the primacy of the Pope over the entire Church, and the infallibility of the Pope when speaking *ex cathedra*[4]. This occurs when the Pope issues a solemn proclamation of dogma on matters of faith and morals regarding the entire Church, which must be adhered to by all Catholics under pain of excommunication. In practice, this power has only been exercised once since the First Vatican Council, when Pope Pius XII wrote *Munificentissimus Deus* in 1950 to define the Assumption of Mary.

At the time of its publication, however, the First Dogmatic Constitution caused a great deal of concern regarding its potential for abuse. It was not universally accepted even within the Church itself, and several German Catholic communities broke with Rome and became known as the Old Catholics. The conflict between Church and State flared up in many countries

---

[4] From the chair.

during this time period, but the struggle in the German Empire was perhaps the highest profile. It was here that the Protestant Reformation was born, and it was here that a new revolution was beginning to unfold.

Chancellor Otto von Bismarck of the German Empire was a firm Lutheran, and he saw this declaration of infallibility as having great potential for abuse. Furthermore, much of the Catholic population in the southern areas of the Empire had recently sided with Austria in a losing war against Prussia, and many members of the aristocracy perceived them as a potential internal threat during future conflicts. In July of 1871, he directed the Prussian Ministry of Culture to merge its Catholic and Protestant sections, ostensibly to ensure *"the exclusively political attitude of equal justice for all."* In the same year, the Pulpit Law prohibited the use of homilies to further political objectives.

In the following March, the School Supervision Act eliminated Church oversight of the Prussian public school system and prohibited clergy from participating in education. The Jesuits Law was passed in June of 1872 and banned all Jesuit institutions from the German Empire. In response, the Vatican rejected the German ambassador to the Holy See and, in response to *that*, Prussia suspended all diplomatic relationships with Rome.

At this point, statesman and scientist **Dr. Rudolf Virchow** observed, *"Ich habe die Überzeugung, es handelt sich hier um einen großen Kulturkampf"* – loosely translated, *"I'm of the belief that this is a great culture war."* This phrase, *Kulturkampf*, was quickly adopted to describe the ongoing period of struggle.

In 1873, the Prussian Constitution was amended to subject the Church to civil authority. The May Laws allowed for religious disaffiliation – any citizen could stand before a Justice of the Peace, reject their Church membership, and free themselves from any dues owed to the Church. Regulations were also levied on excommunication and the training and appointment of clergy.

Pope Pius IX quickly condemned this *Kulturkampf* in his encyclical *Etsi multa*. He also condemned its connection to Freemasonry:

> *Some of you may perchance wonder that the war against the Catholic Church extends so widely. Indeed, each of you knows well the nature, zeal, and intention of sects,* **whether called Masonic or some other name.** *When he compares them with the nature, purpose, and amplitude of the conflict waged nearly everywhere against the Church, he cannot doubt that the present calamity must be attributed to their deceits and machinations for the most part. For from these* **the synagogue of Satan** *is formed, which draws up its forces, advances its standards, and joins battle against the Church of Christ.*

Why was Freemasonry dragged into this condemnation? Freemasonry, or part thereof, was actively involved in it. Faced with waning membership and growing social unrest, the German Grand Lodges decided to mold themselves as the exemplar of civic responsibility. This extended beyond self-improvement into an active and protracted campaign to improve society itself. The Vatican's attempts to maintain its traditional power over this society was seen as a direct threat to the freedom of its citizens.

At this time, **Johann Caspar Bluntschli** was serving as the Grand Master of the *Großloge zur Sonne*[5]. Bluntschli was a Swiss statesman who had immigrated to Bavaria in 1847, following an upheaval in Switzerland, and quickly became involved in international politics. In 1873 he made the following argument against the Catholic Church during a speech to his Lodge:

> *Should the progress that humanity has made over the centuries be preserved? If humanity wants to rescue its own progress, then it must defend itself against this terrible power, which attempts to undermine that progress with every permissible and impermissible means.* **Masonry itself must assume the intellectual dimension of this battle in the service of humanity.** *It would be condemned if it did not fulfill this task.*

In 1874, he made the following declaration at the *Großlogenbund*[6]:

> *It is a professional duty for the lodges to see to it, that the brethren become fully conscious of the relations of Freemasonry to the sphere of ethical life and cultural purposes. Freemasons are obliged to put into effect the principles of Freemasonry in practical life and to defend the ethical foundations of human society, whensoever these are assailed.* **The Federation of the German Grand Lodges will provide, that every year**

---

[5] The Grand Lodge of the Sun.
[6] The German Grand Lodge League.

questions of actuality be proposed to all lodges for discussion and uniform action.

This innocuous sentence was cited by many members of the Church, of the Fraternity, and of the public at large as evidence that the German Lodges were actively debating the *Kulturkampf* and making proposals for additional reforms. Bluntschli and others would later attempt to unite all of the German Grand Lodges under one national Grand Lodge for the expressed purpose of taking an even more active role in social and political activism, reshaping the *Großlogenbund* into a cohesive presiding organization. However, continuing struggles between conservative and liberal factions prevented this union from solidifying.

The struggle between Church and State also continued to churn. The Prussian Civil Registry Law of 1874 asserted civil authority over birth, marriage and death records. The Expatriation Law imposed penalties of exile on clergy performing religious duties without government oversight and approval. In August of 1874, Eduard Kullman attempted to assassinate Chancellor Otto von Bismarck in Bad Kissingen. Bismarck escaped with a gunshot wound to the hand. Kullman declared that Church law required his actions, and was sentenced to 14 years hard labor.

In 1875, the Breadbasket Law required clergy to pledge their support of civil authority or forfeit government subsidies. The Congregation Law expanded the prohibition of the Jesuits to include all religious orders, except those that cared for the sick. The Church Finances Administration Law required that all Church property be administered by a democratically-elected civil council within each parish. The Old-Catholic Church Entitlement Law granted access to Church properties and cemeteries to the Old Catholics.

Finally, in 1876, all Church assets were formally placed under government supervision. Any clergy that refused to conform were exiled.

This struggle was not limited only to the German Empire. In 1877, the *Grand Orient de France* removed the Landmark for a belief in a supreme being. Recognition between Grand Lodge jurisdictions has always been fraught with politics and difficulties in communication, which only increased as Freemasonry spread around the world and into different cultures. The Landmarks are a mutually-recognized list of characteristics to help Grand Lodges determine which of their fellows are operating in proper form, and which are not.

Prohibiting atheism has long been one of these requirements. In response to its removal, the United Grand Lodge of England (UGLE) withdrew recognition of the *Grand Orient de France*. The majority of American and British Empire jurisdictions followed the UGLE. The majority of continental European jurisdictions, with the notable exceptions of Germany and Scandinavia, followed the Grand Orient.

Up until this point, the Fraternity had mostly coexisted as one big, dysfunctional Masonic family. When the contemporary critics of this time period directed their ire against Freemasonry as a whole, it was because the Fraternity was still something of a whole when much of this conflict occurred. This was not the first schism to divide the Fraternity, but it is the longest-lasting and (save for a brief reconciliation following the First World War) continues to this day. The nuances of Masonic recognition are not always understood by outsiders and many assume that Freemasonry remains more universal than it actually is. The rights and, particularly, the wrongs of one particular branch of the Fraternity tends to paint the whole in the popular view.

Thus, in 1884, Pope Leo XIII again condemned Freemasonry and its association with the *Kulturkampf* in *Humanum genus*:

This twofold kingdom St. Augustine keenly discerned and described after the manner of two cities, contrary in their laws because striving for contrary objects; and with a subtle brevity he expressed the efficient cause of each in these words: "Two loves formed two cities: the love of self, reaching even to contempt of God, an earthly city; and the love of God, reaching to contempt of self, a heavenly one." At every period of time each has been in conflict with the other, with a variety and multiplicity of weapons and of warfare, although not always with equal ardour and assault. **At this period, however, the partisans of evil seems to be combining together, and to be struggling with united vehemence, led on or assisted by that strongly organized and widespread association called the Freemasons. No longer making any secret of their purposes, they are now boldly rising up against God Himself.**

Shortly afterward, the wind abruptly changed. Socialism was on the rise in Europe, and both the religious and civil establishments felt threatened enough to unite once again against a new common enemy. In 1886, the First Peace Law abolished state exams for clergy, relaxed the earlier education and civil registry laws, and reestablished Church disciplinary powers. In 1887, the Second Peace Law relaxed the ban on religious orders. The Jesuits, however, remained banned.

Pope Leo XIII, in an Allocution delivered on 23 May 1887, then summarized: *"By the law just passed, as you are aware, former laws were in part abrogated, in part greatly mitigated; and at last an end has been made of that terrible conflict, which, while it ground down the Church, did no good to the state."*

Some branches of Freemasonry, however, continued their struggle. For example, in 1904, Louis Andre, the French Minister of War and a member of the *Grand Orient de France*, recruited Masonic groups to keep tabs on army officers and to report if any attended mass. He maintained a system of note cards, on which each officer was identified with *"Corinth"* or *"Carthage"*. Corinthians were to be promoted. Carthaginians - the Catholics - were to be held back.

Jean Bidegain, Assistant Secretary of the *Grand Orient de France,* sold a batch of these cards to a right-wing nationalist organization. The resulting scandal (*L'Affaire des Fiches de délation*, or "the Affair of the Cards of Denunciation") resulted in the resignation of the French Prime Minister in 1905. Thus, modern conspiracy theories such as the rumored Masonic interference in England's Metropolitan Police Service ring with a faint echo of unfortunate historical truth.

The popular theory for the repression of Freemasonry, by both religious and civil authorities, is often distilled to a conflict between toleration and tradition or tyranny. This may be true to some extent, but human interaction is not this simple.

From some perspectives there may be significant doctrinal conflicts with the teachings and traditions of Freemasonry. One of the core tenets of the Fraternity is to focus on what people in common rather than on how they differ, and suggests that one can be a good person regardless of which specific religion one follows. Thus, the concepts of morality and spirituality are differentiated – the definition of the latter being reserved for religion, but the former being the duty of all humanity. Rotary International was similarly denounced by the Catholic Church in 1928 for proposing a nonsectarian concept of morality, but did not suffer the same lasting repression. Philosophical differences often obscure more practical concerns – unlike Rotary, Freemasonry had garnered a reputation for actively antagonizing the Church in temporal affairs.

Likewise, Freemasonry on the European continent maintained a reputation not just for its support of democracy, but also for directly meddling in civil affairs well into the lead-up to the First World War. When totalitarianism swept across Europe in the interbellum years, the Fraternity was subjected to significant civil repression for more than just its fundamental ideals – it was specifically targeted as a driver of political and social revolution in these countries. This history of activism would prove to be a much more existential threat to these burgeoning dictatorships than mere philosophy.

Pope Pius IX

Chancellor Otto von Bismarck

Dr. Rudolf Virchow

Between Berlin and Rome.

"Admittedly, the last move was unpleasant for me; but the game still isn't lost. I still have a very beautiful secret move."

"That will also be the last one, and then you'll be mated in a few moves – at least in Germany."

Johann Caspar Bluntschli
Grand Master
Grand Lodge of the Sun
German Grand Lodge League

LOGE LIBERTÉ CHÉRIE: A LIGHT IN THE DARKNESS

"OF ONE MIND." (FOR ONCE!)

The Dripping of the Cards

Cries the F∴ – *Mercy, do not throw any more! We are submerged!!...*

NIGHT AND FOG

Repression of Freemasonry in Europe came swiftly as totalitarian regimes took power. Each time a regime annexed or invaded new territory, the local Freemasons found themselves on the wanted list. Many Grand Lodge jurisdictions ceased operations and went underground, and some never recovered.

Adolf Hitler singled out Freemasonry as a tool of a worldwide Jewish conspiracy in *Mein Kampf*. He wrote in Chapter 11, "Race and People":

> *To strengthen his political position he [the Jew] tries to tear down the racial and civil barriers which for a time continue to restrain him at every step. To this end he fights with all the tenacity innate in him for religious tolerance -* **and in Freemasonry, which has succumbed to him completely, he has an excellent instrument with which to fight for his aims and put them across. The governing circles and the higher strata of the political and economic bourgeoisie are brought into his**

nets by the strings of Freemasonry, and never need to suspect what is happening.

Only the deeper and broader strata of the people as such, or rather that class which is beginning to wake up and fight for its rights and freedom, cannot yet be sufficiently taken in by these methods. But this is more necessary than anything else; for the Jew feels that the possibility of his rising to a dominant role exists only if there is someone ahead of him to clear the way; and this someone he thinks he can recognize in the bourgeoisie, in their broadest strata in fact. The glovemakers and linen weavers, however, cannot be caught in the fine net of Freemasonry; no, for them coarser but no less drastic means must be employed. **Thus Freemasonry is joined by a second weapon in the service of the Jews: the press.** *With all his perseverance and dexterity he seizes possession of it. With it he slowly begins to grip and ensnare, to guide and to push all public life, since he is in a position to create and direct that power which, under the name of 'public opinion,' is better known today than a few decades ago.*

[…]

The general pacifistic paralysis of the national instinct of self-preservation begun by Freemasonry in the circles of the so-called intelligentsia is transmitted to the broad masses and above all to the bourgeoisie by the activity of the big papers which today are always Jewish. *Added to these two weapons of disintegration comes a third and by far the most terrible, the organization of brute force. As a shock and storm* *troop, Marxism is intended to finish off what the preparatory softening up with the first two weapons has made ripe for collapse.*

Hermann Göring was made Minister President of Prussia in 1933. The Grand Lodges operating in the region met with him in 1934, and afterwards he concluded that *"there is no room for Freemasonry in the National Socialist State"*. Members began to flee the Fraternity in fear of persecution until the Grand Lodges closed in 1935 ahead of a police deadline.

The Gestapo then confiscated all Lodge materials and records, including membership lists. These rolls were used to identify and arrest Freemasons, even those who had abandoned their membership. Temple furniture, working tools, and other materials were displayed in Anti-Masonic Exhibitions held in Munich in 1937 and Paris in 1942. An estimated 65,000 German Freemasons were murdered over the course of the war.

This cycle of abolishment, seizure of identifying records, and subsequent arrest would be repeated in countries across Europe as the Third Reich expanded. The Gestapo entered Belgium in May of 1940 prepared with 2,000 dossiers on notable Freemasons. Subsequently, the *Grand Orient de Belgique*[7] was officially dissolved. In August of 1940, approximately 179 crates of Masonic records, artwork, and furniture were shipped to Germany.

This repression was not limited to theft. In 1938, the Masters of the Lodges in Vienna were deported to concentration camps, including Dachau. Grand Master

---

[7] Grand Orient of Belgium.

Hermannus van Tongeren of the Grand Orient of the Netherlands was arrested and died on 29 March 1941 in the Sachsenhausen concentration camp. Grand Master **Philotas Pappageorgiou** of the Grand Lodge of Greece was also imprisoned and died from complications of his mistreatment in 1947.

The prosecution of Freemasonry was only a small facet of a much larger Fascist agenda.

The predecessor of these programs was the Black Reichswehr, an extralegal paramilitary organization founded during the Weimar Republic and which operated in tandem with the *Femegerichte*, a secret court system[8]. These courts tried and convicted *in absentia* known informants for the Military Inter-Allied Commission of Control, instituted to enforce the Versailles Treaty on defeated Germany. Those convicted were marked by the *Arbeits-Kommandos*[9] for execution. This labor group was ostensibly founded to support civilian building projects, but instead functioned as an unofficial extension of the German Army to circumvent limitations on German troop strength. In practice, the *Arbeits-Kommandos* were responsible for murdering German citizens tried and convicted in these secret courts without their knowledge.

In 1921 the activities of the Black Reichswehr were revealed by the German pacifist **Carl von Ossietzky**, who later became a vocal opponent of the policies and activities of the Nazi Party. Adolf Hitler came to power in January of 1933 and one month later, on 28

---

[8] Originally this term referred to vigilante courts that operated in Germany during the Middle Ages. The modern German idiom is the equivalent of a "kangaroo court".

[9] Work-Commandos.

February, Ossietzky was arrested. After imprisonment and torture at the Esterwegen concentration camp, an International Red Cross representative described him as *"a trembling, deadly pale something, a creature that appeared to be without feeling, one eye swollen, teeth knocked out, dragging a broken, badly healed leg… a human being who had reached the uttermost limits of what could be borne."*

He contracted tuberculosis in 1936 and was transferred to a hospital in Berlin-Charlottenburg for treatment. Later that year he was awarded the Nobel Peace Prize. Fredrik Stang, Chairman of the Nobel Committee, defended this controversial award in his award ceremony speech given on 10 December 1936:

Let me point to only one noteworthy fact: no less than six previous recipients of the Nobel Peace Prize have lent their support to Ossietzky's candidacy for the award.

But, many people ask, has Ossietzky really contributed so much to peace? Has he not become a symbol of the struggle for peace rather than its champion?

In my opinion this is not so. But even if it were, how great is the significance of the symbol in our life! In religion, in politics, in public affairs, in peace and war, we rally round symbols. We understand the power they hold over us. Moreover, as a rallying point, a symbol may well be preferable to a personality. Men can all too often be compared to the "holder", the wicked Norwegian fairy, beautiful when looked at from the front, but hollow in the back. Such is not the case with the symbol because the symbol is born of an idea and is the bearer of an idea. It exists through the idea which first created it and reflects it faithfully and without distortion.

We have among our poems a few lines about a symbol, lines which are quoted more and more frequently:

> *For that is the great thing and the sublime thing, that the banner may wave, though the man has to die.*

The symbol certainly has its value. But Ossietzky is not just a symbol. He is something quite different and something much more. He is a deed; and he is a man.

Carl von Ossietzky succumbed to his illness on 4 May 1938 in Berlin-Pankow at 48 years of age.

A similar program was instituted on 7 December 1941 when *Generalfeldmarschall* Wilhelm Keitel, Chief of the Armed Forces High Command, issued a directive targeting resistance cells, activists, politicians, intellectuals, and other perceived enemies of the National Socialist State. The accused were to be sent to Germany for trial in secret courts, thus bypassing military and judicial procedure. These activities focused on Belgium, France, Luxembourg, Norway, Denmark, and the Netherlands. The directive read as follows:

> *Directives for the prosecution of offences committed within the occupied territories against the German State or the occupying power, of 7 December 1941.*
>
> *Within the occupied territories, communistic elements and other circles hostile to Germany have increased their efforts against the German State and the occupying powers since the Russian campaign started. The amount and the danger of these machinations oblige us to take severe*

measures as a deterrent. First of all the following directives are to be applied:

I. *Within the occupied territories, the adequate punishment for offences committed against the German State or the occupying power which endanger their security or a state of readiness is on principle the death penalty.*

II. *The offences listed in paragraph I as a rule are to be dealt with in the occupied countries only if it is probable that sentence of death will be passed upon the offender, at least the principal offender, and if the trial and the execution can be completed in a very short time. Otherwise the offenders, at least the principal offenders, are to be taken to Germany.*

III. *Prisoners taken to Germany are subject to military procedure only if particular military interests require this. In case German or foreign authorities inquire about such prisoners, they are to be told that they have been arrested but that the proceedings do not allow any further information.*

IV. *The Commanders in the occupied territories and the Court authorities within the framework of their jurisdiction, are personally responsible for the observance of this decree.*

V. *The Chief of the High Command of the Armed Forces determines in which occupied territories this decree is to be applied. He is authorized to explain and to issue executive orders and supplements.*

The Reich Minister of Justice will issue executive orders within his own jurisdiction.

Reichsführer-SS Heinrich Himmler further explained this directive to the Gestapo on the day it was issued:

After lengthy consideration, it is the will of the Führer that the measures taken against those who are guilty of offenses against the Reich or against the occupation forces in occupied areas should be altered. The Führer is of the opinion that in such cases penal servitude or even a hard labor sentence for life will be regarded as a sign of weakness. **An effective and lasting deterrent can be achieved only by the death penalty or by taking measures which will leave the family and the population uncertain as to the fate of the offender.** *Deportation to Germany serves this purpose.*

One week later, *Generalfeldmarschall* Keitel issued his interpretation in accordance with Directive V:

Efficient and enduring intimidation can only be achieved either by capital punishment or by measures by which the relatives of the criminals do not know the fate of the criminal. The prisoners are, in future, to be transported to Germany secretly, and further treatment of the offenders will take place here; these measures will have a deterrent effect because: A. The prisoners will vanish without a trace. B. No information may be given as to their whereabouts or their fate.

This program would become known as the *Nacht-und-Nebel-Erlass*, or Night and Fog Decree, as its victims appeared to vanish into thin air. The overall goal was to keep the occupied territories pacified by fear without directly implicating Germany in criminal conduct or treaty violations. It is estimated that 6,639 people from France alone were arrested, interrogated, tortured, and imprisoned or executed in the four years between 1941 and 1944.

LOGE LIBERTÉ CHÉRIE: A LIGHT IN THE DARKNESS

Hermannus van Tongeren
Grand Master
Grand Orient of the Netherlands

Philotas Pappageorgiou
Grand Master, Grand Lodge of Greece

Carl von Ossietzky on his arrival at Esterwegen, 1933.

Generalfeldmarschall
Wilhelm Keitel

An American soldier examines markings on prisoners' clothing in Natzweiler-Struthof, marked with a large X and the letters *n n* for *Nacht und Nebel* (Night and Fog).

THE PRIESTS OF ESTERWEGEN

The logistics of forcibly relocating such a large number of people are enormous, and the Night and Fog prisoners were not sent directly to their final destinations. Many Belgian political prisoners passed through the *Emslandlager*, a series of 15 labor, punitive, and prisoner-of-war camps on the border with the Netherlands. This penal system served as a temporary waypoint and holding area between their capture and their final imprisonment deeper in German territory.

Emslandlager VII (Esterwegen) was isolated on all sides by peat bogs. The main section of the camp consisted of two rows of barracks. In the middle was a gallows for attempted escapees, nicknamed "The Red Square" or "Moscow Square". The barracks were surrounded a 20-foot-tall barbed wire fence and four guard towers.

The barracks were divided by walls into three interior rooms and were entered through a mud room with two sets of locked doors. At the front of each barrack was a work room containing two rows of five tables, with two wooden benches on either side of each table for 14 seats. The tables were each placed against the wall with small barred windows for light. Behind each bench was a tall row of cabinets with a tin box for each prisoner, which separated the tables into alcoves. At the end of the corridor was a rudimentary stove that was fed with a few meager rations of peat to heat the barrack.

In the center of the barrack was a large dormitory with metal-framed bunk beds, with bundles of straw laid over wooden boards to sleep on. In the back was a small washroom with a cold water tap running between two toughs and a single bucket to serve as a latrine.

Each barrack housed over a hundred prisoners. Half of the camp prisoner population were German criminals, who were forced to labor in the surrounding peat bogs. The other half were *Nacht und Nebel* political prisoners, including soldiers, partisans, civil servants, doctors, lawyers, journalists, priests, teachers, students, craftsmen, aristocrats, and other intellectuals that were deemed dangerous by Nazi ideology. Their labor was to sort ammunition and radio components.

The political prisoners were only allowed to leave the barracks for one half-hour supervised walk. Their food was of such poor quality (only about 1,000 calories per day) that the prisoners lost about 9 pounds of body weight per month as they slowly starved to death. When Esterwegen closed in May of 1944, only 95 prisoners had died within its walls. This was scarcely a rounding error in comparison to what followed.

During work hours, guards would make surprise inspections on each barrack, beating any prisoners not in their assigned seats with batons. Other guards would bring leashed dogs, who were trained to attack the legs of fleeing escapees. A system quickly developed within the barracks in which certain prisoners would stand watch for the arrival of the guards, warning the others to return to their seats and avoid punishment.

The prisoners found many different ways to keep their spirits up and their minds active. Some took to engaging in friendly, but sometimes heated debates with each other. Others provided lectures on their careers or hobbies. There were several professional and amateur playwrights, songwriters, and musicians to entertain and boost morale. Still others sought solace in their personal religions and beliefs.

On Sunday mornings, the Catholic prisoners of Barrack № 6 gathered at an empty cartridge-sorting table for Mass. Two priests had been assigned to Barrack № 6. Father Charles Vanden Bosch, nicknamed **Father Agnello** ("little lamb") after his home province, was a Franciscan priest and former military chaplain who had served in World War I.

In August of 1914 the German army launched a devastating attack on the nine forts at Namur. Seven of the forts were quickly taken, and on 25 August the final two surrendered. The defenders of Fort Suarlée withstood over 3,600 artillery hits and all but one 57 mm cannon had been knocked out of action. With the battlefield obscured by smoke and raining debris, the commanding officer asked of Father Agnello one final task:

You are a priest! You are asked to risk your life before everyone is killed. The enemy is already under the walls! He will fall on us! I fear an incredible massacre, as frightful as it is useless. Try to go out to offer our surrender!

Rather than wave the white flag, Father Agnello donned his vestments and walked towards the enemy line while holding his chalice above his head, prompting the attacking soldiers to seize fire. He was captured by the Germans and conscripted to serve as a stretcher bearer, as his eyesight was failing from exposure to mustard gas and he could serve no other useful purpose. After the war, Father Agnello was decorated for his actions at Namur but would fully lose his vision.

Forced to give up his dreams of being a missionary due to his disability, Father Agnello dedicated himself anew to advocating for the blind. First he memorized the Latin Mass, and then learned Braille, the piano, and the violin. In 1922 he founded *l'Institut pour Aveugles de guerre*[10]. Father Agnello went on to create an institute for disabled and blind children in Flanders and a nursery school for children of the blind in Namur.

After Belgium was occupied in 1940, Father Agnello joined the *Comète*[11] resistance movement and served to hide an illegal radio transmitter in his school library. He was arrested on 9 July 1942 after another member of his cell was discovered, and he was then transferred to Esterwegen in July of 1943. He was such a burden on the guards that they allowed a fellow prisoner to help him around. The two of them were also given uncharacteristic permission to walk relatively freely within the prisoner area of the camp, which provided them the opportunity to pass messages between the various barracks.

---

[10] The Institute for the Blind of the War.
[11] Comet.

Father Agnello was transferred to the "Parish Block" of Dachau in the winter of 1945. He was tortured by being forced to stand outside in subzero temperatures for several hours. He contracted pneumonia as a result and died on 9 March 1945, at 62 years of age. His remains were repatriated to Belgium in 1962 and laid to rest with honors in the cemetery of Woluwe-Saint-Pierre.

The prisoner that Father Agnello chose to assist him was a fellow priest, **Father Jean-Joseph Marie Heymans**. Father Heymans hailed from a family of industrialists from the area surrounding Brussels. His family temporarily fled to England to escape the First World War, but his father returned to Belgium out of patriotism to prevent the Germans from using his soap factory to produce glycerin as a raw material for explosives.

Father Heymans studied history, philosophy, and literature at the Leo XIII Seminary and theology at the Grand Seminary of Malines. He was ordained on 26 December 1929 and, after a brief stint as a professor at Notre Dame de Cureghem, he became a vicar at the parish of Sainte-Familie in Woluwe-Saint-Lambert

In 1933 his parish founded a Scout Unit[12], and Father Heymans served as their Chaplain. Though he was not himself a Scout prior to this, he was still given a totem – according to Scouting tradition in France and Belgium, this is a unique nickname that describes the personality of each Scout. Father Heymans was given the totem *Pélican impétueux*, or Impetuous Pelican. To be impetuous is act decisively and fearlessly, and the pelican is symbolic of one who sacrifices himself

---

[12] Later renamed the 42nd Unit Jean Heymans in his memory.

unquestioningly for those that he loves[13]. This totem was certainly an appropriate choice as he quickly became known for his selflessness and generosity to all men, regardless of race, religion, or political leanings.

Father Heymans mobilized with the Belgian Army on 26 August 1939 as a Chaplain, Second Class. After the capitulation of the government, like many others he became involved in the Belgian Resistance movement. He assisted refugees fleeing to France or England, found families to shelter Jewish children, provided dropboxes for Resistance communications and documents, and housed an English radio operator who passed along news of the War and messages from the Belgian government-in-exile in London.

Farther Heymans was arrested by the Gestapo on 15 May 1942 and exactly one year later he arrived at the prison of Saint Gilles. Military officers were treated much better than the rest of the population. This included the privilege to write to his family once every 15 days.

At Saint Giles he learned that he had been betrayed by his sister, Elizabeth, but in his letters he expressed that his situation was better than many others. He wrote to his brother and his wife:

> *My dear Joseph, my dear Adeline, dear little nieces and nephews, I have it very difficult. I'm still tough. But so many other men in prison have it much harder. They are the dads.*

---

[13] The Dalmatian pelican will press its lower bill against its chest to empty its throat sack, which has a bright red interior during mating season. Observations of this behavior at a distance gave rise to the medieval legend that, in times of scarcity, the pelican will pierce its own chest and give its lifeblood to feed its young.

Father Heymans was also very concerned that the political prisoners typically did not have priests among them to care for them spiritually. He wrote that it was better to truly serve as a priest, than to live in luxury and opulence while others suffered. He also wrote that a man who has not suffered himself cannot console others, and that he was thankful to God for giving him the perspective necessary to empathize with and minister to his fellow prisoners. Father Heymans requested to be transferred to the general population, but was refused. In response he resigned his military rank so that, without it, he could be reclassified as a political prisoner rather than a prisoner of war.

In his final letter to his brothers, Philippe and Joseph, he wrote:

> *I can die in 1943 as in 1953. So, between men and brothers, here is my testament: Love one another as I have loved you; it is not a small amount. Where I go, you will come one day to join me. Bear your crosses as, with thanks to God, I have tried to bear mine. I kiss the cross of my Lord and give a kiss to the whole family. Goodbye, Philippe, Joseph, and the whole family. I forgive Elizabeth for her mistakes. What I have in the bank is for the poor. The rest is for the family.*
>
> *Your brother who loves you and is very happy under his cross,*
>
> *Jean*

While the military officers were sent to Dachau, Father Heymans was instead transferred to Esterwegen, where he met Father Agnello. He was later moved to the prison at Bayreuth and finally to the concentration camp at Flossenbürg. He died of typhoid fever twenty-two days later on 15 April 1945, one week before the camp was liberated. He was 40 years old.

The third priest of Esterwegen was **Father Éduoard Froidure**. During the First World War, Father Froidure served in the Belgian Army as a soldier assigned to the 101st Battery, Group III, 6th Artillery Regiment. After the war he studied philosophy and literature, before joining the same Leo XIII Seminary as Father Jean Heymans. The two priests became good friends and shared many experiences - they were ordained by the same Cardinal, served at neighboring parishes, and both helped to create Scout Units.

Father Froidure returned to duty as a chaplain with the Belgian Army Air Force in 1939. He fled to France with the Belgian government in 1940, where his unit was assigned a secret mission by Prime Minister Hubert Pierlot to move the gold reserves of the National Bank to England ahead of the German advance. After Pierlot and his government evacuated to London, Father Froidure returned to Belgium and joined the Resistance. His first operation was designated *Paquets brûlés*[14], in which he helped fleeing resistance fighters with aliases and new documentation.

After several close calls, Father Froidure was arrested by the Gestapo at 7 in the morning on 9 October 1942 while he was preparing for Mass. A search of his property uncovered 5 tons of contraband food, which he had been distributing to needy children in the area. Father Froidure was first imprisoned at

---

[14] Burned Packages

Saint Giles with Father Heymans, where he was brutally tortured by being stripped, bound wrist and ankle, and forced to stand bent over at the waist until he lost his balance. The guards then fell upon him with batons.

As with many Night and Fog prisoners, he was transferred through several more facilities during his imprisonment, including Esterwegen, Börgermoor, and finally at Dachau. At Esterwegen, Father Froidure was confined mostly to Barrack № 9, designated as the camp infirmary[15], but due to his medical experience he was allowed to visit several other barracks as well. During this time he was once again reunited with Father Heymans, and also became good friends with Father Agnello.

Father Froidure was rescued during the American liberation of Dachau and later administered the last rites for Father Agnello at his internment. He was tragically killed at the age of 72 by a hit-and-run driver in Watermael-Boitsfort on 10 September 1971. In his memoirs about his experiences at Esterwegen, he recounted that:

"The spirit of understanding and tolerance of non-practitioners allows the mass to be recited aloud and partly sung."

What Father Froidure had observed was a growing camaraderie between the prisoners of Esterwegen. In some instances, non-Catholics were ensuring the privacy of the Mass and respectfully limiting

---

[15] Very little medical attention was provided to prisoners by the camp doctors. In practice, the infirmary was where sick prisoners were merely sent to die.

disruptions. In others, they were actively providing some measure of protection and security from the sudden arrivals of the guards. This grew into a very special symbiosis within the community of Barrack № 6.

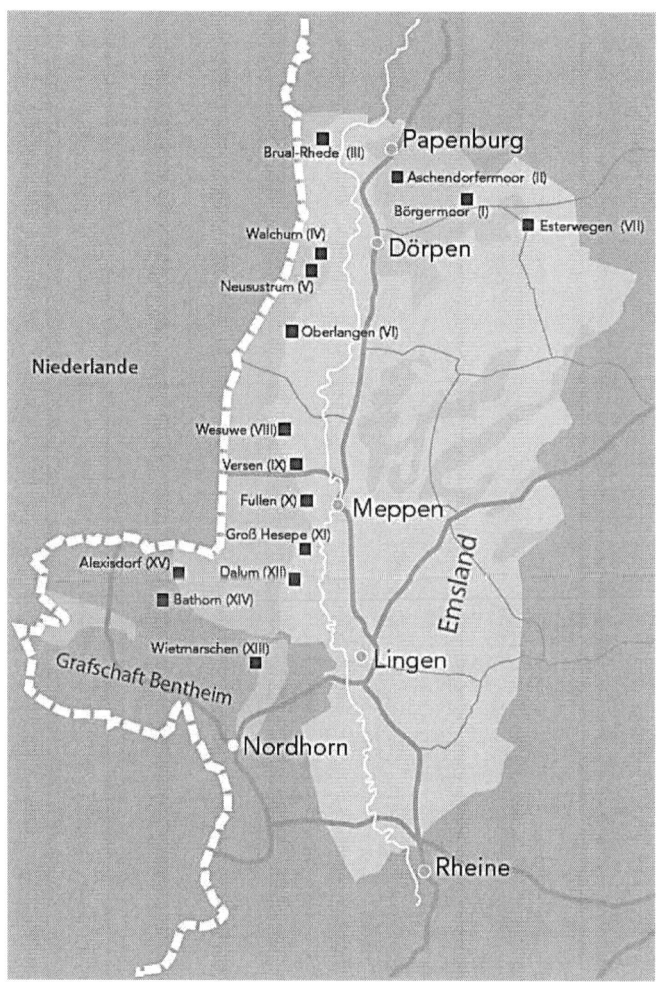

The *Emslandlager* concentration camp system.

LOGE LIBERTÉ CHÉRIE: A LIGHT IN THE DARKNESS

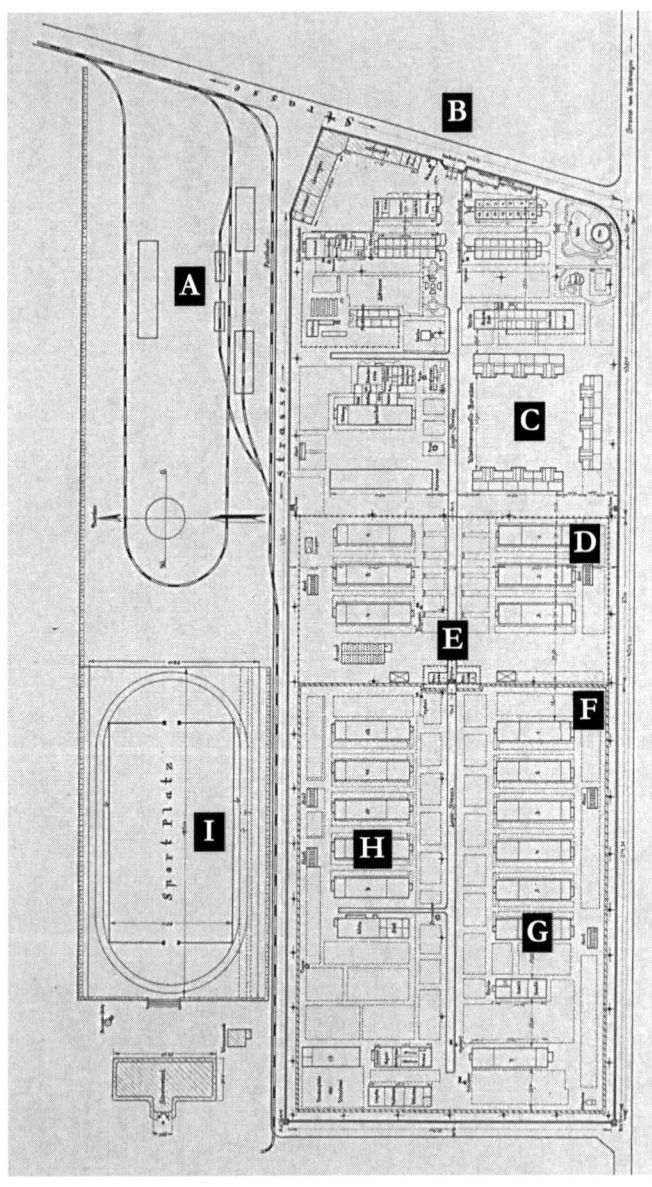

Opposite page: The layout of the Esterwegen (Emslandlager VII) concentration camp.

Points of interest:

- A   Rail depot for transporting prisoners
- B   Front gate
- C   Administrative offices
- D   Barracks for criminal prisoners
- E   Gate into political prisoner area
- F   Barracks for political prisoners
- G   Barrack № 6
- H   Barrack № 9
- I   Track and playing field

LOGE LIBERTÉ CHÉRIE: A LIGHT IN THE DARKNESS

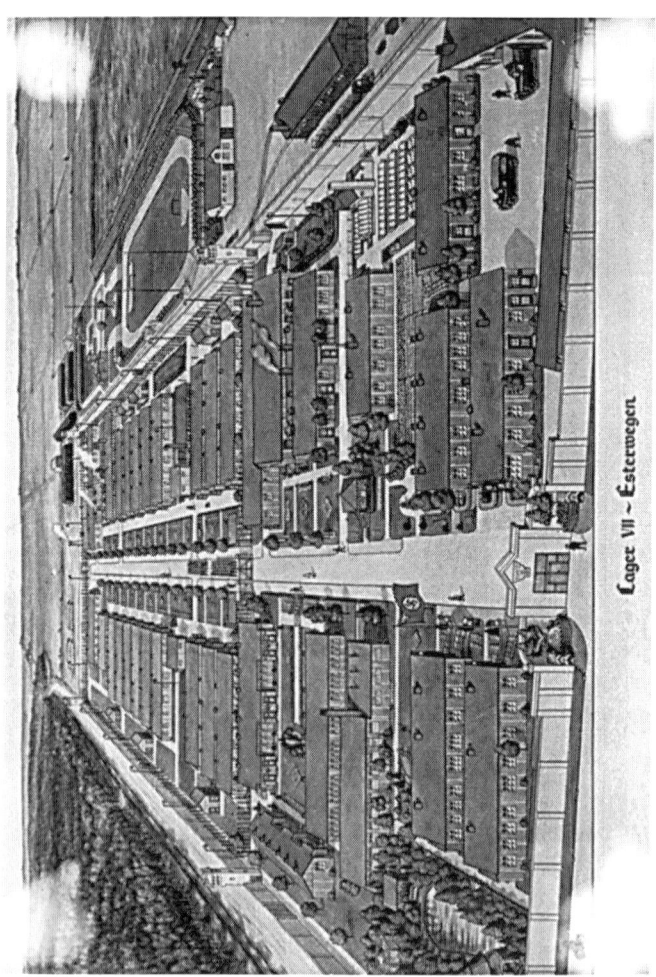

A drawing of the Esterwegen concentration camp circa 1944.

This drawing was sourced from a souvenir photo album of Erich Mitschkle, one of the camp guards.

LOGE LIBERTÉ CHÉRIE: A LIGHT IN THE DARKNESS

The layout of Barrack № 6.

Points of interest:

- A   Entry room
- B   Work room
- C   Table where Catholics and Freemasons both met
- D   Dormitory
- E   Washroom

"The Barracks" by Fernand Van Horen

Father Agnello Vanden Bosch

Father Jean Heymans

Father Éduoard Froidure

LOGE LIBERTÉ CHÉRIE

Among the non-practitioners protecting the gathering Catholics in Barracks № 6 were four Freemasons of the Grand Orient of Belgium. They came to refer to themselves as *couvreurs*[16] – the French equivalent of the English *tiler* or *tyler*. The Tyler is an officer who traditionally sits outside of closed-door Lodge meetings with a drawn sword to ward off eavesdroppers. In practice, he verifies that all attendees are Masons in good standing, handles late arrivals, and keeps wayward members of the public from blundering into meetings and embarrassing themselves.

At Esterwegen, these self-appointed *couvreurs* put aside their centuries-old animosity with the Catholic Church and rose to the occasion to stand watch for Father Agnello, Father Heymans, and their fellow prisoners. In return for their help, the Catholics stood

---

[16] A literal translation of the English title, meaning roofer, shingler, slater, or tile-layer.

watch while the Freemasons used the same table to meet in a "circle of Fraternity", which was at first merely a discussion group.

Dr. Franz Rochat and **Jean Sugg**, longtime friends and colleagues, arrived at Barrack № 6 on 21 May 1943. Rochat was a university professor, pharmacist, and director of Laboratories Optima in Brussels and had been arrested on 28 February 1942. Sugg was a pharmaceutical representative and had been arrested on 21 March 1942. Both were contributors to *La Voix des Belges*[17], a resistance newsletter during the occupation, and both were also members of *Loge Les Amis philanthropes*[18].

Sugg in particular was a translator of German and Swiss texts, and he also helped downed bomber crews and provided money and food stamps to people who avoided forced labor. Upon arrival as Esterwegen, he was put to work assisting the camp administrators. This gave him access to both the camp records and the confiscated belongings of the prisoners. Sugg used this access to scavenge parts and build a crystal radio receiver, after which he translated Radio London broadcasts for his fellow prisoners.

Guillaume "Guy" Hannecart arrived at Barrack № 6 one week later, on 28 May 1943. He was a lawyer, a poet, and a writer of four novels and fifteen plays. He put his literary skills to use in overseeing *La Voix des Belges* and applied his theatrical abilities to serving as Master of *Loge Les Amis philanthropes*. Guy Hannecart thus worked closely with both Dr. Franz Rochat and Jean Sugg, and he had been arrested on 27 April 1942

---

[17] The Voice of the Belgians.
[18] Philanthropic Friends.

for serving in the national leadership of the Belgian Resistance. During his captivity at Esterwegen, he continued to write plays on scraps of toilet paper for the amusement of his fellow prisoners.

Judge Paul Hanson arrived at Esterwegen with Guy Hannecart. He was a Justice of the Peace in the canton of Louveigné-Grivegnée and a member of *Loge Hiram*[19]. On 23 February 1942 he presided over civil suit brought by the collaborationist *Corporation Nationale de l'Agriculture et de l'Alimentation,* (CNAA)[20] against 121 local farmers for not paying an annual shakedown fee of 75 Belgian Francs[21]. A farmer, by the CNAA definition, was any person who owned at least a single cow.

The CNAA arrived at court with armed thugs to impress upon the judge what his verdict should be. Judge Hanson threw out the thugs and, in a fiery speech on the sanctity of rule of law, he denied the legality of the CNAA itself and fined them instead. Despite initial attempts by the official Belgian press to suppress news of this event, a report by Radio London spread the news across the occupied territory. This ruling made Judge Hanson both famous in Belgium and infamous in Germany, and he was arrested two months to the day of his verdict on 23 April 1942.

In the fall of 1943, three more Freemasons were assigned to Barrack № 6:

Luc Somerhausen arrived on 12 October 1943. He was a reporter covering the Belgian Senate and a member of the *Service de Renseignement et d'Action*

---

[19] Named for a key figure in Masonic allegory.
[20] The National Corporation of Agriculture and Food.
[21] Equivalent to approximately $26 USD (2019), converted with the contemporary exchange rate and adjusted for inflation.

(SRA)[22]. Somerhausen was also a member of *Loge Action et Solidarité*[23] and the Deputy Secretary of the *Grand Orient de Belgique*. He passed his time in the barrack by teaching oratory to his fellow prisoners by holding debates on various topics. In particular, he served as a calming influence when tensions flared between the diverse groups housed in Barrack № 6.

Dr. Laurent-Joseph Degueldre arrived on 15 October 1943. He had been arrested on 29 May 1943 for serving as a Section Chief for *L'Armée secrete*[24]. Unbeknownst to the Gestapo, at the time of his arrest Laurent-Joseph and his wife Maria (also a doctor) were also hiding Rose Micmacker, a 17-year-old Jewish woman, in their home by pretending that she was their housekeeper. Dr. Degueldre was a member of *Loge Le Travail*[25] in Verviers, but spent most of his time at Esterwegen with his fellow resistance fighters than with the growing group of Freemasons. Because of this, he is often and unfortunately left out of many accounts of this story.

Dr. Degueldre was known for his singing voice, and for the bawdy songs that he improvised to keep up morale in the barrack. He also gave Guy Hannecart the affectionate nickname "the emperor with the flowery beard" for his magnificent facial hair and his resemblance to Leopold II. Unfortunately, Hannecart would later be forced to shave by the guards.

Dr. Amédée Miclotte, Ph.D. arrived on 22 November 1943. He was a secondary teacher in Vorst and a Section Chief of the SRA with Luc Somerhausen.

---

[22] The Intelligence and Action Service.
[23] Action and Solidarity.
[24] The Secret Army.
[25] The Work.

He was a member of *Loge Les Vrais Amis de l'union et du progrès réunis*[26] and had been arrested on 29 December 1942.

With seven members[27] the assembled Freemasons could constitute a new Lodge. Luc Somerhausen, as the former Deputy Grand Secretary, had experience with the proper procedure and adapted it as well as he could to the circumstances. He also suggested the name *Liberté chérie* for this new Lodge. The typical translation of this common French idiom into English is "cherished Liberty". However, the French language is rich with deeper meaning and this simple translation does not do the name justice. This is a personal address of a man to his beloved. It's affectionate, it's intimate, and it perfectly describes her members' undying love and unyielding hope for freedom.

Though Luc Somerhausen never revealed his inspiration, there are two common theories. The first is that it was a reference to the sixth verse of *La Marseillaise*, the French national anthem:

> *Amour sacré de la Patrie,*
> *Conduis, soutiens nos bras vengeurs*
> **Liberté, Liberté chérie,**
> *Combats avec tes défenseurs !*
> *Sous nos drapeaux que la victoire*
> *Accoure à tes mâles accents,*
> *Que tes ennemis expirants*
> *Voient ton triomphe et notre gloire !*

---

[26] The True Friends of Union and Progress Reunited.
[27] The minimum number necessary to constitute a Lodge under the *Grand Orient de Belgique*.

Sacred love of the Fatherland,
Lead, support our avenging arms
Liberty, cherished Liberty,
Fight with thy defenders!
Under our flags may victory
Hurry to thy manly accents,
So that thy expiring enemies
See thy triumph and our glory!

The more likely theory is that it was a reference to the *Chant des Marais*[28]. This famous prison song was written in the Börgermoor (Emslandlager I) concentration camp in 1933 and quickly spread throughout the Emslandlager penal system. Many Night and Fog prisoners had been kept at Börgermoor temporarily before being transferred to Esterwegen, and they brought this song with them. It was later popularized in German under the name *Die Moorsoldaten*[29]. The third and fourth verses are as follows:

Bruit des pas et bruit des armes
Sentinelles jours et nuits
Et du sang, des cris, des larmes
La mort pour celui qui fuit

Mais un jour dans notre vie
Le Printemps refleurira
Liberté, Liberté chérie
Je dirai tu es a moi

---

[28] The Song of the Marsh.
[29] The Peat Bog Soldiers.

Footsteps and the sound of weapons
Sentinels days and nights
And blood, screams, tears
Death for the one who flees

But one day in our life
Spring will bloom again
Liberty, cherished liberty
I will say that you are mine

Loge Liberté chérie began its work on 28 November 1943 by electing officers. Judge Paul Hanson was elected to serve as Worshipful Master, the presiding officer of the Lodge, in deference to his reputation as a fair judge and leader. Luc Somerhausen served as Senior Warden, the first vice president and responsible for maintaining harmony among the members. Dr. Franz Rochat served as Secretary and Dr. Amédée Miclotte as Orator, who were responsible respectively for keeping records of their meetings and providing (or arranging for) lectures on topics of interest.

The new officers wrote themselves a charter, but none were skilled enough to draw a tracing board. This form of Masonic artwork consists of a collage of symbols, such as the working tools of a stonemason, that is used as a visual aid when explaining the teachings of the Fraternity to a new member. In the tradition of many Masonic jurisdictions, including Belgium, the tracing board is displayed at all times that a Lodge is open and is one of its necessary items of furniture. The members of *Loge Liberté chérie* approached an artist in a neighboring barrack, Fernand Van Horen, and asked him to create such a drawing with only vague details and no explanation as to what he was producing.

Van Horen was born in the Democratic Republic of Congo, then the Belgian Congo, and was repatriated to Brussels in 1912 following the death of his father. He studied at the *Académie royale des beaux-arts de Bruxelles*[30] and became a popular cartoonist for the newspaper *Le Soir* in 1936 under the *nom de guerre* of Horn.

After briefly serving as the first black reserve officer of a Belgian cavalry regiment (the 2nd Lancers) in 1940, Van Horen joined the Secret Army on 1 March 1941. He was arrested by the Gestapo on 24 February 1943 and passed through Esterwegen before finally arriving at Flossenbürg. Van Horen spent his time in the camps drawing portraits of his fellow prisoners on scraps of paper. He was present with Father Jean Heymans when the priest passed away in 1945 and was rescued by soldiers commanded by General George Patton on 23 April 1945. After the war, Van Horen resumed his successful career as a cartoonist and passed away on 15 September 2005 at the age of 95.

The first meeting of *Loge Liberté chérie* served as their installation of officers. During their following meetings the assembled Freemasons focused on philosophical discussions, including the symbols of the Great Architect of the Universe[31], the future of Belgium after the war, and the role of women in the Fraternity.

---

[30] The Royal Academy of Fine Arts in Brussels.
[31] The Great (or Grand) Architect of the Universe is not a specific deity or "Masonic God". This term is used rhetorically by Freemasons to refer to the divine in a general sense and serves as a placeholder for the personal deity of each individual Freemason.

Within a few months, additional members joined the Lodge:

Colonel Jean-Baptiste De Schrijver arrived on 7 February 1944. He had served as Cabinet Chief of the Ministry of Defense in 1940 and was a member of the *Loge La Liberté* in Ghent. He had been arrested on 2 September 1943 for espionage and possession of weapons. Colonel De Schrijver was quickly elected as Junior Warden of *Loge Liberté chérie*. This officer, equivalent to a second vice president, is traditionally responsible for looking after the well-being of Lodge members between meetings.

On 20 February 1944, the Lodge initiated **Fernand Erauw** into the Fraternity. He was a secretary of the Court of Auditors and a grenadier reserve officer in the Belgian Army. Erauw had been arrested as a member of the Belgian resistance, escaped imprisonment, was recaptured, and arrived at Esterwegen with Guy Hannecart and Judge Paul Hanson. Luc Somerhausen described the Degree:

> *I actively participated in a ceremony that, to be as simple as it was clandestine[32], consisted of taking in the profane[33] Fernand Erauw, who had been proposed to join the founders, and who had agreed to the proposal. This ceremony, to which secrecy the community of priests had been asked to help, and which received help from us in their prayers, took place around one of the dining tables,*

---

[32] This use of the word "clandestine" refers to the common definition, in that the meeting was kept secret and hidden from the guards.
[33] This usage of "profane" is not to denote irreverence or disrespectfulness, but in its Masonic context as someone who is not a member of the Fraternity.

following a very simplified ritual, the individual components of which were explained to the newcomer and he henceforth participated in the work of the Lodge.

Fernand Erauw expressed his awe at the ceremony and that there was much to take in. He also recounted that, as is the case with many candidates, he remembered very few specifics of the explanations but that the experience itself left a favorable and lasting impression.

Unfortunately, this brief happiness was not to last long. Luc Somerhausen was transferred out of Esterwegen on 22 February 1944, shortly after Fernand Erauw was initiated. Colonel Jean-Baptiste De Schrijver followed on 15 March 1944. However, on 18 March 1944, **Henri Story** arrived at the camp. He was an industrialist, and served as an alderman in Ghent and the Master of *Loge Le Septentrion*[34]. He was a member of many resistance groups and a Captain of the SRA with Miclotte and Somerhausen. In particular, he served as their point of contact with England. Story had been arrested on 20 October 1943 and was to be the tenth and final member of *Loge Liberté chérie*.

The camp at Esterwegen was permanently closed on 23 May 1944. The eight remaining Freemasons were then scattered to other concentration camps and *Loge Liberté chérie* ceased to exist. Before dispersing, the charter and tracing board were buried in a tin box at the roots of a nearby tree during one of their walks so that they could be recovered after the war.

Judge Paul Hanson was transferred to a prison in the city of Essen. Essen was bombed by the Allies on

---

[34] The North, in Masonic tradition a place of ignorance.

26 March 1944 and Hanson perished in the rubble of the prison. He was 55 years old.

Dr. Franz Rochat was transferred to Untermansfeld and died there on 6 January 1945. He was 37 years old.

Henri Story, **Dr. Amédée Miclotte**, and **Colonel Jean-Baptiste De Schrijver** were transferred to Groß-Rosen. Story died there on 5 December 1944 at the age of 47. Dr. Miclotte was reported missing on 8 February 1945, having been seen last in the camp infirmary. He was 42 years old. Colonel De Schrijver died the following day, on 9 February 1945, at the age of 51.

Guillaume Hannecart was transferred to Bergen-Belsen and was executed by cyanide injection on 25 February 1945. He was 41 years old.

Jean Sugg was transferred to Buchenwald and died there on 6 May 1945, two days before the end of the war in Europe. He was 48 years old.

Dr. Laurent-Joseph Degueldre was transferred to Ichtershausen prison and survived a death march later that spring. He was then put onto a work detail locating and exhuming unexploded bombs for disposal. His detail escaped on 11 April 1944, was rescued by the U.S. Army Air Forces four days later, and was finally repatriated to Belgium on 7 May 1945. Dr. Degueldre passed in Pepinster on 19 April 1981, surrounded by his family, at the age of 78. For their efforts in protecting Rose Micmacker, Laurent-Joseph and Maria Degueldre were posthumously honored as "Righteous Among the Nations" (№ 12244) by the State of Israel in 2011.

Luc Somerhausen was transferred to the Oranienburg Sachsenhausen concentration camp on

22 February 1944. A few months later the camp was bombed by the Allies, and the surviving prisoners were tasked with clearing the rubble. During a work shift Somerhausen paused to catch his breath and didn't notice an SS guard approaching. The guard called him a *"damned Jew"*, stuck him across the face, and knocked his glasses off. Another nearby prisoner stopped to pick them up, who turned out to be **Fernand Erauw**. They were in such poor condition that at first they didn't recognize each other.

After this, the two remained inseparable through a death march in the spring of 1945 until they were rescued on 4 May 1945 by the Red Army and hospitalized at Saint-Pierre's in Brussels on 21 May 1945. Upon rescue, Luc Somerhausen was noted to suffer from *"nervousness, extreme weight loss, tachycardia, pleuritic joint, scurvy, double perforation of the eardrum, and decreased visual acuity and memory."* Fernand Erauw stood just over 6 feet tall, but upon his rescue only weighed 70 pounds.

Dr. Laurent-Joseph Degueldre, Luc Somerhausen, and Fernand Erauw were the only surviving members of *Loge Liberté chérie*. Though this Lodge never worked again, its story was not quite over yet.

LOGE LIBERTÉ CHÉRIE: A LIGHT IN THE DARKNESS

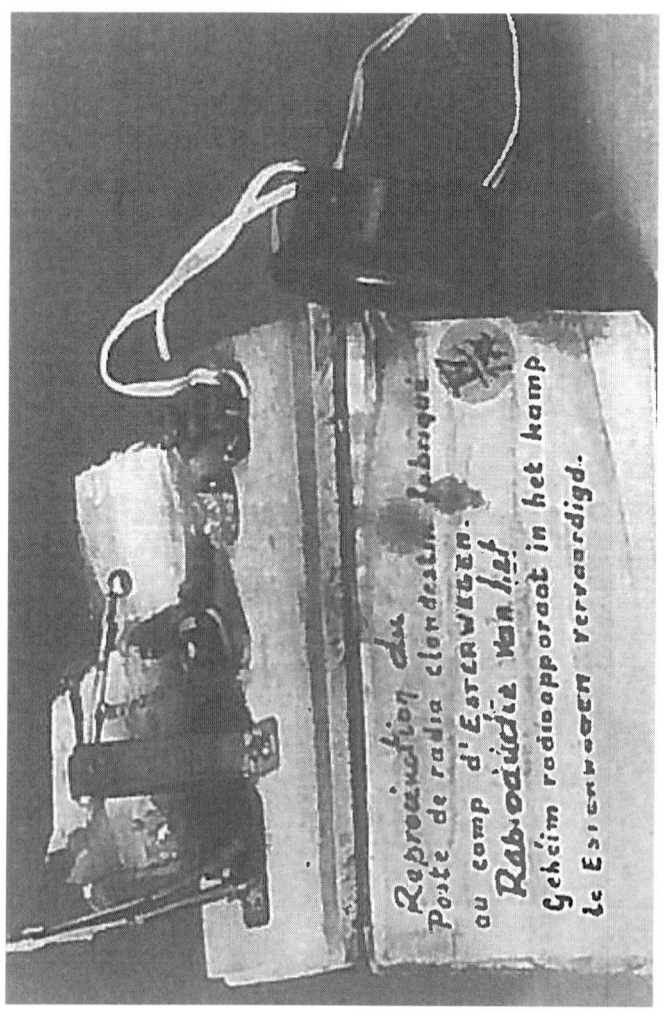

A reproduction of the crystal radio fabricated clandestinely by Jean Sugg.

LOGE LIBERTÉ CHÉRIE: A LIGHT IN THE DARKNESS

Guillaume Hannecart

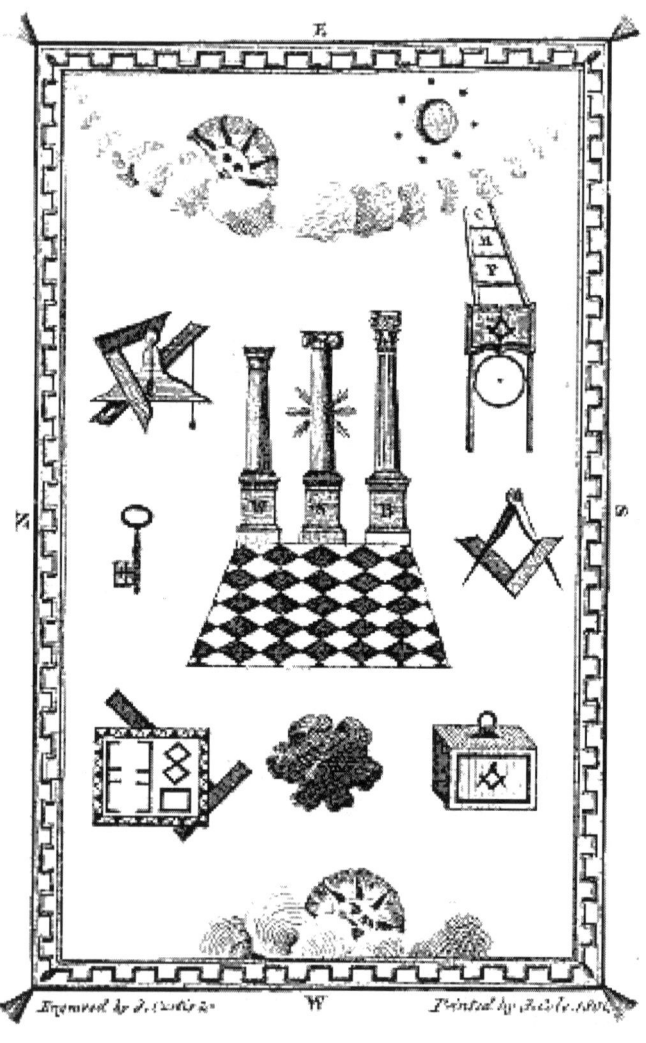

Tracing board depicted in an early Masonic exposé, 1801.

Self-portrait of Fernand "Horn" Van Horen

Henri Story

Memorial to Colonel Jean-Baptiste De Schrijver.

REMEMBRANCE

On 13 November 2004, a memorial was dedicated by Belgian and German Freemasons. Created by architect Jean de Salle, it consists of prison bars breaking upon a rough ashlar[35] of granite. The memorial sits on a mosaic pavement of alternating light and dark stone.

The plaque reads:

This memorial was erected in memory of 8 Masonic members of the Belgian resistance movement[36] who in 1943/44 were imprisoned in Esterwegen (Camp VII) in the block of foreign "Night and Fog" prisoners in Barrack No.6.

---

[35] A rough-sided, unfinished stone.
[36] As previously detailed, *Loge Liberté chérie* had 10 members over its brief existence. Fernand Erauw was discounted here for reasons that will be explained. Dr. Laurent-Joseph Degueldre was also neglected, which is unfortunately common in many accounts of the history of this Lodge.

LOGE LIBERTÉ CHÉRIE: A LIGHT IN THE DARKNESS

Under the most difficult conditions, they founded and gave life to the Masonic lodge "Liberté Chérie", a unique occurrence in the history of National Socialist concentration camps.

Loge Liberté chérie was not the only Lodge to form in the concentration camps. *Loge L'Obstinée*[37] was formed by captured Belgian Army officers in the Oflag X-D prisoner-of-war camp near Hamburg. *Loge Les Frères Captifs d'Allach*[38] was created as a French-speaking international Lodge in Allach, an annex of Dachau near Munich. Very little history of these Lodges survived the war. However, the story of *Loge Liberté chérie* was kept alive due to the passionate efforts of her survivors.

In August of 1945, Luc Somerhausen sent a detailed report on *Loge Liberté chérie* to the Grand Master of the Grand Orient of Belgium. He continued to champion the formal recognition of *Loge Liberté chérie*, but his treatment during the war left him with severe memory loss and Somerhausen experienced great difficulty in recounting an accurate history of its members and activities.

The existence of *Loge Liberté chérie* would prove to be a bureaucratic nightmare for the Grand Orient of Belgium. On one hand, it was held to be an undisputed example of Masonic principles in action. On the other, it was technically clandestine[39].

---

[37] The Obstinate, or stubborn.
[38] The Captive Brothers of Allach.
[39] In Masonic context, a clandestine Lodge is one formed and operated without the expressed consent of the Grand Lodge or Orient of its jurisdiction. This consent is typically documented in a charter, dispensation, or warrant issued by the governing body. *Loge Liberté chérie* had written itself its own charter.

In November of 1945 the Grand Orient of Belgium met for its first annual communication[40] since it was dissolved in 1940, and the delegates were deeply divided on the topic of formal recognition. One recommended to address *Loge Liberté chérie* in the tradition of a military Lodge, which are traditionally formed on a temporary basis and were not typically recognized formally. Another argued that formal recognition would set a dangerous precedent for truly clandestine Lodges that may have formed while the disbanded Grand Orient of Belgium was not able to maintain its jurisdiction. Some delegates felt that formal recognition was entirely unnecessary to confirm the legitimacy of the Lodge, while still others felt that a failure to recognize the Lodge would be a tremendous insult to the survivors and a travesty against the Fraternity itself.

Recognition of *Loge Liberté chérie* would be approved on 18 November 1945 with only two abstentions. However, the actual work to effect this recognition was not completed. Luc Somerhausen and Fernand Erauw made a painful pilgrimage back to Esterwegen in 1946 in an attempt to recover the charter and formally legitimize *Loge Liberté chérie*. They found that the Germans had since demolished the entire site, leaving only a few dilapidated shacks in a bare field. The British had then repurposed the site to serve as a prison for war criminals awaiting trial. Even the trees had been cut down and removed, and the tin box containing the Lodge records and materials could not be found.

---

[40] An annual meeting in which delegates from the various subordinate Lodges meet to elect Grand Lodge officers, vote on legislation, charter new Lodges, and handle other matters of importance relevant to the entire jurisdiction.

Similarly, the story of *Loge Liberté chérie* faded into obscurity for many years.

Luc Somerhausen returned to his work with the Belgian Senate, but he never fully recovered from the war and suffered from memory difficulties for the rest of his life. He joined the Communist Party in 1948 but was expelled in 1954. He continued working as President of the Belgian Committee of the *Fédération Internationale des Résistants* (FIR)[41], an association of veterans and former anti-Axis resistance fighters. He denounced the organization in 1957 for its overt bias in favor of the Eastern Bloc, resulting in a violent attack perpetrated by some of its members.

Fernand Erauw continued his Masonic journey and was accepted by *Loge Balder*[42]. However, given the lingering questions regarding the recognition of *Loge Liberté chérie* and the unconventional manner of his initiation, it was decided that this ceremony was invalid and would have to be repeated. This very much angered Luc Somerhausen, who was greatly insulted by the references to his worthy apprentice as being profane[43]. Erauw, however, was not discouraged and welcomed the opportunity to experience his initiation a second time. He later settled down with his wife Nina, a fellow Night and Fog survivor of the Ravensbrück concentration camp, and continued his career in teaching finance law at the Free University of Brussels.

Luc Somerhausen passed on 5 April 1982 at the age of 79. Following the funeral, Erauw met with

---

[41] International Federation of Resistance Fighters – Association of Anti-Fascists.
[42] Named for the Norse god of light and purity.
[43] See footnote 33.

Somerhausen's son and took up his mentor's self-imposed duty to keep the memory of *Loge Liberté chérie* alive. The sitting Grand Master of the Grand Orient of Belgium in 1986 was teaching in the same department as Erauw, and the two began to meet every Friday morning to chat. The lingering issue of formal recognition for *Loge Liberté chérie* eventually arose.

These discussions culminated on 22 October 1987, when the 249 delegates of the Grand Orient voted unanimously to grant a retroactive charter for *Loge Liberté chérie*. The Lodge was to be placed between № 28 and № 30. It was not itself numbered, as № 29 was reserved by *Loge Simon Stevin*[44], which had transferred from the Grand Orient to the Grand Lodge of Belgium[45] but kept its number reserved in case it returned in the future. Because of this procedural complication, *Loge Liberté chérie* continued to be left off of the formal roll of Lodges of the Grand Orient, much to Fernand Erauw's consternation. Eventually, *Loge Liberté chérie* would be granted № 29bis[46] and *Loge L'Obstinée* would be granted № 29ter[47].

In his later years, Fernand Erauw wrote many articles for the Grand Orient's magazine and in 1993 he published a book on his experiences, titled <u>L'odyssée De Liberté Chérie</u>[48]. He said of his departed brethren:

---

[44] Named for the Flemish mathematician who, among many other achievements, first demonstrated the gravitational constant *g* in 1586, three years before Galileo Galilei.
[45] Several Belgian Lodges made this transfer, as the Grand Lodge of Belgium (at the time) maintained a relationship with the larger community of English or "regular" Freemasonry. Refer to the earlier discussion on page 12.
[46] Equivalent to the second № 29 or № 29B.
[47] The third № 29 or № 29C.
[48] The Odyssey of *Liberté Chérie*.

They did what they should;
They were angry at the iniquity that was captivity;
They raised their voices with strength to destroy these
evils and regain their freedom;
And they acted by trying to do good, to work to the
happiness of humanity!

He passed as the last surviving member of *Loge Liberté chérie* on 8 April 1997 at the age of 83.

The modern story of *Loge Liberté chérie* was also transmitted by fellow Esterwegen survivor **Franz Bridoux**, then a 19-year-old resistance fighter and imprisoned as a member of Dr. Laurent-Joseph Degueldre's section of the Secret Army. He remained close to Dr. Degueldre during their time at Börgermoor and Ichtershausen, and later escaped alongside him and several other prisoners in April of 1944.

Franz Bridoux was not then a Freemason, being underage at the time of his imprisonment, but he later joined the Fraternity in 1966. He would go on to write many books on his experiences in during the war and continued to champion the memory of *Loge Liberté chérie* for the rest of his life. In the forward of his final book, <u>*Liberté Chérie – In Nacht und Nebel*</u>, Bridoux wrote:

"Our hope is that the memory of the founders of the Lodge 'Liberté chérie' will keep us awake to stand in the way of the recurring dangers."

Franz Bridoux passed on 14 January 2017 at the age of 93.

LOGE LIBERTÉ CHÉRIE: A LIGHT IN THE DARKNESS

Memorial dedicated to *Loge Liberté chérie* at Esterwegen.

LOGE LIBERTÉ CHÉRIE: A LIGHT IN THE DARKNESS

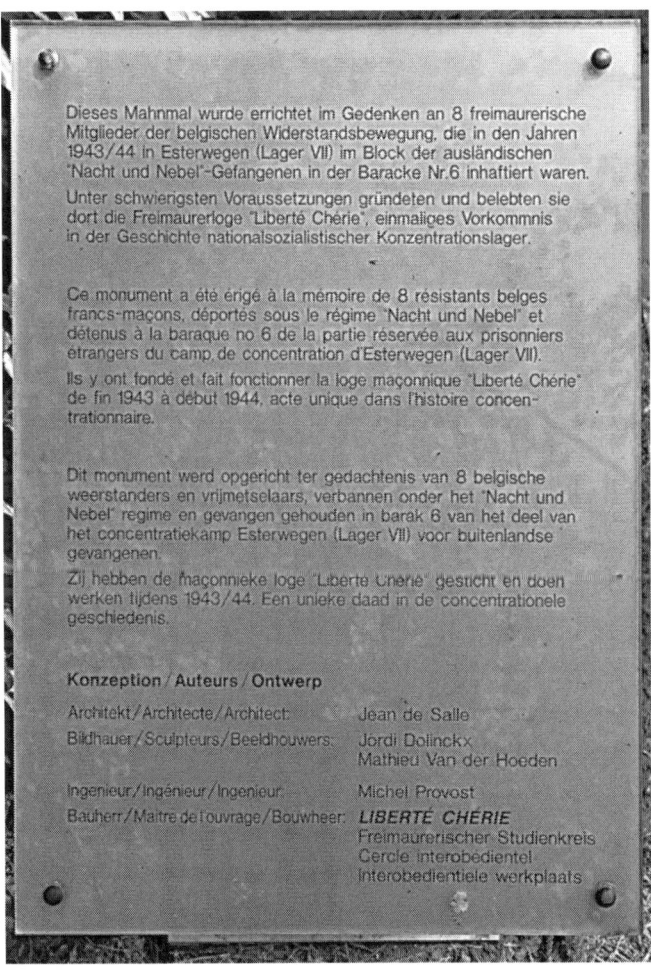

Memorial plaque dedicated to *Loge Liberté chérie* at Esterwegen, translation on page 74.

LOGE LIBERTÉ CHÉRIE: A LIGHT IN THE DARKNESS

Survivors of Esterwegen.

Dr. Laurent-Joseph Degueldre is in the front row on the far right.

Franz Bridoux is standing behind him in the second row, second from right.

LOGE LIBERTÉ CHÉRIE: A LIGHT IN THE DARKNESS

Fernand Erauw (standing) speaking to the *Confédération Nationale des Prisonniers Politiques et Ayant Droits* (National Confederation of Political Prisoners and their Heirs, or CNPPA) in 1975.

Luc Somerhausen is seated to his left.

LOGE LIBERTÉ CHÉRIE: A LIGHT IN THE DARKNESS

Franz Bridoux, 2009

EPILOGUE

Beyond the ten members of *Loge Liberté chérie*, there were several other Freemasons imprisoned at Esterwegen. Due to their strict confinement to their barracks, they may not have even been aware of each other's presence. They were:

Louis Schmidt was an engineer and the mayor of Etterbeek. He was arrested on 27 April 1942. He was later transferred from Esterwegen to Ereslau, where he died on 3 February 1944. He was 66 years old.

Octave Tiquet was an industrialist who was arrested on 22 April 1942 for espionage. He died on 5 March 1944 of septicemia. He was 68 years old.

Hermann De Clercq was also an industrialist and had been arrested in January of 1943. He was transferred through a number of facilities before he died in Dachau on 12 February 1945. He was 33 years old.

Raymond Volkerick was an engineer for the Ministry of Public Works. He was arrested in October of 1941 for espionage. He was transferred to

Brandenburg where he was executed by guillotine on 8 May 1944. He was 42 years old.

As evidence that justice does sooner or later overtake all injustice, the Night and Fog Decree met its end in Nuremberg. On 8 May 1945, *Generalfeldmarschall* Wilhelm Keitel was sent to the Berlin suburb of Karlshorst to submit the German surrender to the Soviet Union. Five days later he was arrested along with the remnants of the Nazi government and faced the International Military Tribunal (IMT). He was charged with conspiracy to commit crimes against peace; planning, initiating and waging wars of aggression; war crimes; and crimes against humanity.

Justice Robert H. Jackson, who took a leave of absence from the United States Supreme Court to serve as the U.S. Chief of Counsel for the Tribunal, specifically included the Night and Fog Decree among Keitel's crimes. Keitel said in a statement before the Tribunal:

As these atrocities developed, one from the other, step by step, and without any foreknowledge of the consequences, destiny took its tragic course, with its fateful consequences.

The Tribunal rejected his defense of following orders in conformity to the *Führerprinzip*[49] and convicted him on all four counts. Their ruling has since been enshrined in military law:

Superior orders, even to a soldier, cannot be considered in mitigation where crimes as shocking and extensive have

---

[49] The Leader Principle, the fundamental system of authority in the Third Reich which placed the commands of the *Führer* above the law.

been committed consciously, ruthlessly and without military excuse or justification.

Keitel was sentenced to death by hanging, despite his pleas to die as a military officer by firing squad. He was executed at 1:20 AM on 16 October 1946, with *"All for Germany! Germany above all!"* as his defiant final words.

It would be easy, and human, to look upon this history through a lens of death and vengeance. The pain and loss of the Night and Fog prisoners should never be forgotten. However, the true legacy of the brethren of *Loge Liberté chérie* is not how they died, but how they chose to live. In the darkest of circumstances, when it must have seemed that G-d had abandoned them, they still focused on the signs of a merciful deity all around them. In a world torn apart by bloodshed and oppression, they dared to dream of a better future in which this terrible war was merely the past. And, as Nina Erauw would later recount,

In this hell, they remained true to themselves, became friends, and made their own Masonic home by including a man who they had come to know and appreciate. I believe that, through their daily lives, they concretely applied the motto, "Liberty, Egality, Fraternity".

Justice Robert H. Jackson makes his opening statement at the International Military Tribunal, Nuremberg.

LOGE LIBERTÉ CHÉRIE: A LIGHT IN THE DARKNESS

Wilhelm Keitel stands trial at the International Military Tribunal, Nuremberg.

BIBLIOGRAPHY

Abrams, Irwin. "The Multinational Campaign for Carl von Ossietzky." International Conference on Peace Movements in National Societies, 1919-1939, 25-29 Sept. 1991, Stadtschlaining, Austria.
Álvarez y Miranda, José. *Boletín Oficial del Obispado de León* (1928): 500.
"The Art of Fernand "Horn" Van Horen." JewishGen. <https://www.jewishgen.org/ForgottenCamps/Exhib/DrawEng.html>
"Cérémonie funèbre d 3 mars 1946." *Bulletin du Sûpreme Counseil de Belgique* 66 (1948): 7-20.
Anderson, James. *The Constitutions of the Free-Masons. Containing the History, Charges, Regulations, &c. of that Most Ancient and Right Worshipful Fraternity. For the Use of the Lodges.* London: William Hunter, 1723.
Bakels, Floris. *Nacht und Nebel: Night and Fog.* Cambridge: The Lutterworth Press, 1993.
Baron, Anne-Marie. *The Shoah on the Screen – Representing Crimes Against Humanity.* Volume I. Strasbourg: Council of Europe Publishing, 2006.

Bessel, Paul. "U.S. Recognition of French Grand Lodges in the 1900s." *The Transactions of the Scottish Rite Research Society* 5 (1996): 221–244.

Birkhaeuser, Jodocus. "The Late Kaiser and the Kulturkampf." *New Catholic World,* 47 (1888) 232-240.

Bracher, Karl. *The German Dictatorship: The Origins, Structure, and Effects of National Socialism.* Westport: Praeger Publishers, 1970.

Bridoux, Franz. *Liberté Chérie: In Nacht und Nebel.* Leipzig: Salier Verlag, 2015.

Bridoux, Franz. *La Respectable Loge Liberté Chérie au camp de concentration d'Esterwegen.* Brussels: Logos, 2012.

Bridoux, Franz and Teman, Catherine. *Liberté chérie, l'incroyable histoire d'une loge dans un camp de concentration.* Paris: La Boîte à Pandore, 2014.

Bridoux, Franz. *"Nuit et Brouillard" au Camp de concentration d'Esterwegen avec la R∴L∴ "Liberté Chérie".* Rixensart: 2003.

Cerviño y González, Florencio. *Boletín Oficial Eclesiástico del Obispado de Orense* 14 (1928): 223-224.

Congregation for the Doctrine of Faith. "The Primacy for the Succession of Peter in the Mystery of the Church." *L'Osservatore Romano, Weekly Edition in English* 18 Nov. 1998: 5-6.

Conot, Robert. *Justice at Nuremberg.* New York: Harper & Row, 1983.

Cooper, Robert. *The Red Triangle: A History of Anti-Masonry.* Surrey: Lewis Masonic, 2011.

Daschez, Roger. *Histoire De La Franc-Maçonnerie Française.* Paris: Presses Universitaires De France, 2003.

"Degueldre Joseph & Maria (Xhervelle)." *The Righteous Among the Nations Database*. Yad Vashem.

Erauw, Fernand. *L'odyssée De Liberté Chérie*. Brussels: Histoire De La Loge, 1993.

Franklin, James. *Catholic Values and Australian Realities*. Brisbane: Connor Court, 2006.

Froidure, Edouard. *Le Calvaire des Malades au Bagne d'Esterwegen*. Liège: Pax, 1945.

Gérard, Jo. *Interview historique de l'Abbé Froidure*. Brussels: Direct Social Communications, 1987.

Guelff, Pierre. *Sur les pas des Francs-Maçons : Une Franc-Maçonnerie de "terrain"*. Waterloo: Éditions Jourdan, 2010.

Gregory XVI. "Mirari vos." Papal Encyclicals Online.

Gruber, Hermann. "Masonry (Freemasonry)." *The Catholic Encyclopedia*. Vol. 9. New York: Encyclopedia Press, 1913.

"Heymans, Jean-Joseph Marie." *Belgisch Staatsblad*, 151 (1947): 5153.

Heijmans, Pierre. "Jean Heijmans dit "L'Abbe Jean Heymans." 2006. TS. Municipal Archives, Woluwé-Saint-Lambert.

Heijmans, Pierre (assumed). "L'exemple donné à ses neveux par Jean Heijmans." TS. Municipal Archives, Woluwé-Saint-Lambert.

"Histoire de la 42eme Unité Jean Heymans (Les Scouts)." *Les guides de la 38e SAINTE-FAMILLE | Les scouts de la 42e JEAN HEYMANS*. <http://38-42.be/unites/la-42eme-unite-jean-heymans-les-scouts/>

Hitler, Adolf. *Mein Kampf*. Franz Eher Verlag, 1925.

Hoffman, Stefan-Ludwig. *Die Politik der Geselligkeit: Freimaurerlogen in der deutschen Bürgergesellschaft, 1840-1918*. Göttingen: Vandenhöck & Ruprecht, 2000.

Jacquemin, Agnello. *Le père Agnello Vanden Bosch: Franciscain, aveugle de guerre, fondateur de l'Oeuvre Nationale des Aveugles, 1883-1945*. Brussels: ONA, 1993.

Jagush, Gabriel. "Elevator Speeches: Forth Worth, Texas; Tuesday, June 20, 2017." Texan Mason, 2017. <https://www.texanmason.com/2017/06/20/elevator-speeches.html>

Laub, Thomas. *After the Fall: German Policy in Occupied France, 1940-1944*. Oxford: Oxford University Press, 2009.

Leo XIII. "Humanum genus: On Freemasonry." Papal Encyclicals Online.

"Liberté Chérie, eine Loge im Konzentrationslager." *Les Cahiers Bleus* 82 (2015): 13-17.

Mackey, Albert. "Couvreur." *An Encyclopedia of Freemasonry and Its Kindred Sciences*. Vol. 1. Chicago: The Masonic History Company, 1924.

Malonga, Samuel. "Né au Congo en 1909, le grand dessinateur Fernand Van Horen alias « Horn » est décédé en 2005." *Mbokamosika*. 1 Dec. 2016.

Martin, Michael. "Why is Freemasonry so Secret in Britain?" *The Educator*. 2001. <http://theeducator.ca/masonry-secret-britain/>

Martínez y Noval, Bernardo. *Boletín Eclesiástico de la Diócesis de Almería* (1928): 316-319.

Masini, Claudio. *Liberté chérie: Una Loggia Massonica nel Campo di Concentramento di Esterwegen (1943-1944)*. Rome: BastogiLibri, 2016.

McGovern, James. "The Life and Life-Work of Pope Leo XIII." Chicago: Monarch Book Company, 1903.

McManus, John. "Historical Relationship Between the Catholic Church and Freemasons… Why Roman Catholics are Prohibited by the Church from Becoming Freemasons." *The Phoenixmasonry Masonic Museum and Library.* 2009. <http://www.phoenixmasonry.org/Catholic_Church_and_Freemasonry.htm>

Murray, John. "The War between Prussia and Rome." *Quarterly Review* 136.272 (1874): 289-332.

Pahaut, Claire. *Nina Erauw. Je suis une femme libre (1917-2008).* Hainult: Hainaut Culture et Démocratie, 2009.

Parrado y García, Agustín. *Boletín Eclesiástico del Obispado de Palencia* 77 (1928): 391.

Pius IX. "Etsi multa: On the Church in Italy, Germany, and Switzerland." Papal Encyclicals Online.

Pius IX. "Quanta cura: Forbidding Traffic in Alms." Papal Encyclicals Online.

Pius IX. "The Syllabus of Errors." Papal Encyclicals Online.

Pius XII. "Munificentissimus Deus: Defining the Dogma of the Assumption." Papal Encyclicals Online.

Powell, Christopher. "Pure, Ancient Masonry and the Catholic Church." *Ars Quatuor Coronatorum* 132 (2019).

Ruelland, Jacques. "Liberté chérie, Une Loge dans l'univers concentrationnaire nazi." 2008.

Schatz, Klaus. *Papal Primacy: From its Origins to the Present.* Collegeville: Liturgical Press, 1996.

Schiffer, William. "La Loge Liberté Chérie: La Lumière brille dans les Ténèbres, mais les Ténèbres ne l'ont point reçue." *La Gazette de la Fraternité Universelle* (2017).

Šmidrkal, Václav. "The International Federation of Resistance Fighters: Communist anti-fascism, Germany, and Europe." *War Veterans and the World after 1945: Cold War Politics, Decolonization, Memory.* Abingdon: Routledge, 2018.

Somerhausen, Luc. "La R∴L∴ Liberté Chérie." 1945. TS. Grand Orient de Belgique, Brussels.

Somerhausen, Luc. *L'humanisme agissant de Karl Marx.* Paris: Richard-Masse, 1946.

Somerhausen, Luc. "Une Loge Belge Dans Un Camp De Concentration." *Feuillets d'Information Du Grand Orient De Belgique* 73 (1975).

Stang, Fredrik. "Award ceremony speech." NobelPrize.org. Nobel Media AB 2019. <https://www.nobelprize.org/prizes/peace/1935/ceremony-speech/>

Thomas, Christopher. *Compass, Square and Swastika: Freemasonry in the Third Reich.* 2011. Texas A&M University, Ph.D. dissertation.

United States. "Partial Translation of Document L-90." *Nazi Conspiracy and Aggression.* Vol. 7. Washington: GPO, 1946.

"Values of Foreign Moneys." 31 USC. Sec. 129.5. *Federal Register.* Vol. 7, Part 1. Washington: National Archives, 1942.

Van den Abeele, Andries. *De Kinderen van Hiram: Vrijmetselaars en Vrijmetselarij.* Ghent: Roularta Books, 1991.

Van Horen, Fernand. "How a drawing saved my life." JewishGen. <https://www.jewishgen.org/ForgottenCamps/Witnesses/HornEng.html>

Verhas, Pierre. *Liberté Chérie: Une Loge Maçonnique Dans Un Camp De Concentration*. Brussels: Labor, 2005.

Verheyen, Henk. *Het Sanatorium: Herinneringen aan de Nazitijd*. Antwerp: Hadewijch, 1994.

Vermote, Michel. "Luc Somerhausen, 'Agent-prospecteur' in Dienst Van Moskou." *Brood & Rozen* 14 (2009): 41–53.

Wheeler-Bennet, John. *The Nemesis of Power: The German Army in Politics 1918-1945*. London: Macmillan, 1967.

ATTRIBUTIONS

Front Cover   "Box." By Meaghan Herbert.

Page 16   "Pope Pius IX." By George Peter Alexander Healy. Public domain.

Page 17   "Otto von Bismarck." By Jacques Pilartz. Public domain.

Page 18   "Rudolf Virchow." Public domain.

Page 19   "Zwischen Berlin und Rom." By Wilhelm Scholtz. Public domain.

Page 20   "Johann Caspar Bluntschli in späteren Jahren." By Gebrüder Fretz. Public domain.

Page 21   ""Of One Mind." (For Once!)." By Punch, or the London Charivari. Public domain.

Page 22   "La dégoulinade des Fiches." By Fertom. Public domain.

Page 32 "Hermannus van Tongeren." By David S. Owens [CC BY-SA 3.0 (https://creativecommons.org/licenses/by-sa/3.0/de/legalcode)], via Freimaurer-Wiki. Available at https://freimaurer-wiki.de/images/1/13/Hermannus_van_Tongeren_older.jpg. Cropped from original.

Page 33 "Philothas Pappageorgiou Grand Master of the Grand Lodge of Greece 1945." Reprinted with permission of the Denslow Collection of the Missouri Masonic Research Library. Cropped from original.

Page 34 "Carl von Ossietzky." Bundesarchiv, Bild 183-93516-0010 / Unknown / CC-BY-SA 3.0.

Page 35 "Wilhelm Keitel." Bundesarchiv, Bild 183-H30220 / CC-BY-SA 3.0.

Page 36 National Archives and Records Administration, College Park. Public domain. Cropped from original.

Page 47 "2011 ELL Übersichtsplan." Reprinted with permission of Stiftung Gedenkstätte Esterwegen. Cropped from original.

Page 48 "Lageplan: Strafgefangenen – Lager VII, Esterwegen." Reprinted with permission of the Niedersächsisches Landesarchiv, Article NLA OS, K Akz. 2001/039 Nr. 60 H. Cropped from original.

LOGE LIBERTÉ CHÉRIE: A LIGHT IN THE DARKNESS

Page 50   "Esterwegen, Germany, Drawing of the camp." By Erich Mitschke. Reprinted with permission of Yad Vashem. Archival Signature 1477, Album Number FA202/1, Item ID 52093.

Page 51   From the archive of Franz Bridoux. Reprinted with permission of Salier Verlag. Text translated to English.

Page 52   "The Barracks." By Fernand Van Horen. Reprinted with permission of JewishGen.org.

Page 53   "Father Agnello Vanden Bosch." Public domain.

Page 54   "Abbè Jean Heymans, 1938." Reprinted with permission of Emmanuel Everarts of 42nd Unit Jean Heymans, Fédération des scouts Baden-Powell de Belgique.

Page 55   "Edouard FROIDURE born 1899, died 1971, Belgian abbot, social entrepreneur." By Olnnu [CC BY-SA 3.0 (https://creativecommons.org/ licenses/by-sa/3.0/legalcode)] via Wikimedia Commons. Available at https://upload.wikimedia.org/wikipedia/co mmons/1/1a/Edouard_ Froidure_%C2%B01899%2B1971.jpg. Cropped from original.

Page 68   From the archive of Franz Bridoux. Reprinted with permission of Salier Verlag.

Page 69   "Guy Hannecart." From the archive of Franz Bridoux. Reprinted with permission of Salier Verlag.

Page 70   "First Degree Tracing Board." By F. Curtis. Public domain.

Page 71   "Horn par Horn (Autoportrait)." By Fernand Van Horen [CC BY-SA 4.0 (https://creativecommons.org/licenses/by-sa/4.0/legalcode)] via Wikimedia Commons. Available at https://upload.wikimedia.org/wikipedia/commons/2/20/Hornbyhorn.jpg.

Page 72   "Henri Story." From the archive of Franz Bridoux. Reprinted with permission of Salier Verlag.

Page 73   "Aalstmon oude-pupillen - Mai 2008." By Danny Paspont. Reprinted with permission of BEL-MEMORIAL.

Page 80   "Kamp Esterwegen." By Dennis Peeter. Public domain. Cropped from original.

Page 81   "Denkmal für die Loge Liberté Chérie, Begräbnisstätte Esterwegen, Bundesstraße 401 in Esterwegen." By Frank Vincentz [CC BY-SA 3.0 (https://creativecommons.org/licenses/by-sa/3.0/legalcode)] via Wikimedia Commons. Available at https://upload.wikimedia.org/wikipedia/commons/c/c1/Esterwegen_-_B401_-_Begr%C3%A4bnisst%C3%A4tte_-_Libert%C3%A9_ch%C3%A9rie_01_ies.jpg.

LOGE LIBERTÉ CHÉRIE: A LIGHT IN THE DARKNESS

Page 82   From the archive of Franz Bridoux. Reprinted with permission of Salier Verlag.

Page 83   "Fernand Erauw." Photos de la Confédération nationale des Prisonniers politiques et ayants droit de Belgique (CNPPA) : congrès et réunions diverses, [1945-...]. Image n° 216153. Reprinted with permission of Collectie CegeSoma — Rijksarchief (004).

Page 84   "PHOTOS 2009 2 liberté chérie 002." By Pierre Guelff. Reprinted with permission. Cropped from original.

Page 88   United States Holocaust Memorial Museum, courtesy of Gerald (Gerd) Schwab. Cropped from original.

Page 89   "Wilhelm Keitel, IMT, Nuremberg Germany, 1945-1946." By Ray D'Addario, U.S. Army Pictorial Service, World War II. Reprinted with permission of the Robert H. Jackson Center. Cropped from original.

Back Cover   Derivative of a photograph provided by the National Archives and Records Administration, College Park. Public domain.

ABOUT THE AUTHOR

Alexander P. Herbert is first an advocate for truth. This dedication has taken him through such diverse professions as forensic science, pharmaceutical research and development, and spaceflight safety engineering. He is also a proud Freemason of the Grand Lodges of Ohio and Manitoba and a member of the Royal Scofield Society. Alexander lives a quiet life in Bedford, Ohio with his wife Meaghan.

Printed in Great Britain
by Amazon